THE WORLD OF ANIME AND MANGA

ANIME AND MANGA: GENRES AND THEMES

by Danielle L. DeFauw

BrightPoint Press

San Diego, CA

© 2024 BrightPoint Press
an imprint of ReferencePoint Press, Inc.
Printed in the United States

For more information, contact:
BrightPoint Press
PO Box 27779
San Diego, CA 92198
www.BrightPointPress.com

ALL RIGHTS RESERVED.

No part of this work covered by the copyright hereon may be reproduced or used in any form or by any means—graphic, electronic, or mechanical, including photocopying, recording, taping, web distribution, or information storage retrieval systems—without the written permission of the publisher.

LIBRARY OF CONGRESS CATALOGING-IN-PUBLICATION DATA

Names: DeFauw, Danielle L., author.
Title: Anime and manga: genres and themes / by Danielle L. DeFauw.
Description: San Diego, CA: BrightPoint Press, [2024] | Series: The world of anime and manga | Includes bibliographical references and index. | Audience: Grades 7–9.
Identifiers: LCCN 2023041559 (print) | LCCN 2023041560 (eBook) | ISBN 9781678207540 (hardcover) | ISBN 9781678207557 (eBook)
Subjects: LCSH: Manga (Comic books)--Themes, motives--Juvenile literature. | Manga (Comic books)--Stories, plots, etc.--Juvenile literature. | Animated films--Japan--Themes, motives--Juvenile literature. | Animated television programs--Japan--Themes, motives--Juvenile literature. | Literary form--Juvenile literature. | LCGFT: Comics criticism. | Film criticism.
Classification: LCC PN6790.J3 D44 2024 (print) | LCC PN6790.J3 (eBook) | DDC 741.5/952--dc23/eng/20230913
LC record available at https://lccn.loc.gov/2023041559
LC eBook record available at https://lccn.loc.gov/2023041560

CONTENTS

AT A GLANCE	4
INTRODUCTION CONNECTING THROUGH ANIME AND MANGA	6
CHAPTER ONE SHONEN AND SHOJO	12
CHAPTER TWO FANTASY AND ISEKAI	24
CHAPTER THREE SCI-FI AND MECHA	36
CHAPTER FOUR SLICE OF LIFE AND SPORTS	48
Glossary	58
Source Notes	59
For Further Research	60
Index	62
Image Credits	63
About the Author	64

AT A GLANCE

- Anime are films made by animators. Manga are comics made by artists called mangakas.

- Both anime and manga include many titles from a variety of genres.

- Different genres may use similar themes. Common themes are friendship, determination, and the hero's journey.

- Shonen is a genre made for teenage boys. Shojo is made for teenage girls.

- Fantasy is among the most popular genres in anime and manga. Animators and mangakas make the impossible possible for characters in this genre.

- Isekai is a subgenre of fantasy. Characters in isekai wake up and find themselves in a new world.

- The sci-fi genre features advanced technology and takes readers on adventures into the future or to other planets.

- Mecha is a subgenre of sci-fi. Mechanical beings such as giant robots are featured in mecha stories.

- In the slice-of-life genre, characters experience events from everyday life. Audiences often relate to these characters' experiences.

- The sports genre often explores themes of teamwork and competition.

INTRODUCTION
CONNECTING THROUGH ANIME AND MANGA

Juri feels lucky to be the president of his high school's anime and manga club. He turns off the TV as the film *Spirited Away* finishes playing. He and the other members have watched many of Hayao Miyazaki's anime. Digging into different genres, or categories of media, has been an adventure. The group also talks about the themes of each movie. Themes are the topics, subjects, or messages in a story. These discussions allow the group to explore the films' deeper messages. Juri says to the group, "I told you there's nothing like anime."

Manga in the shojo genre usually feature strong female characters. In Fruits Basket, **Tohru Honda learns that a good friend and his family turn into animals when people hug them.**

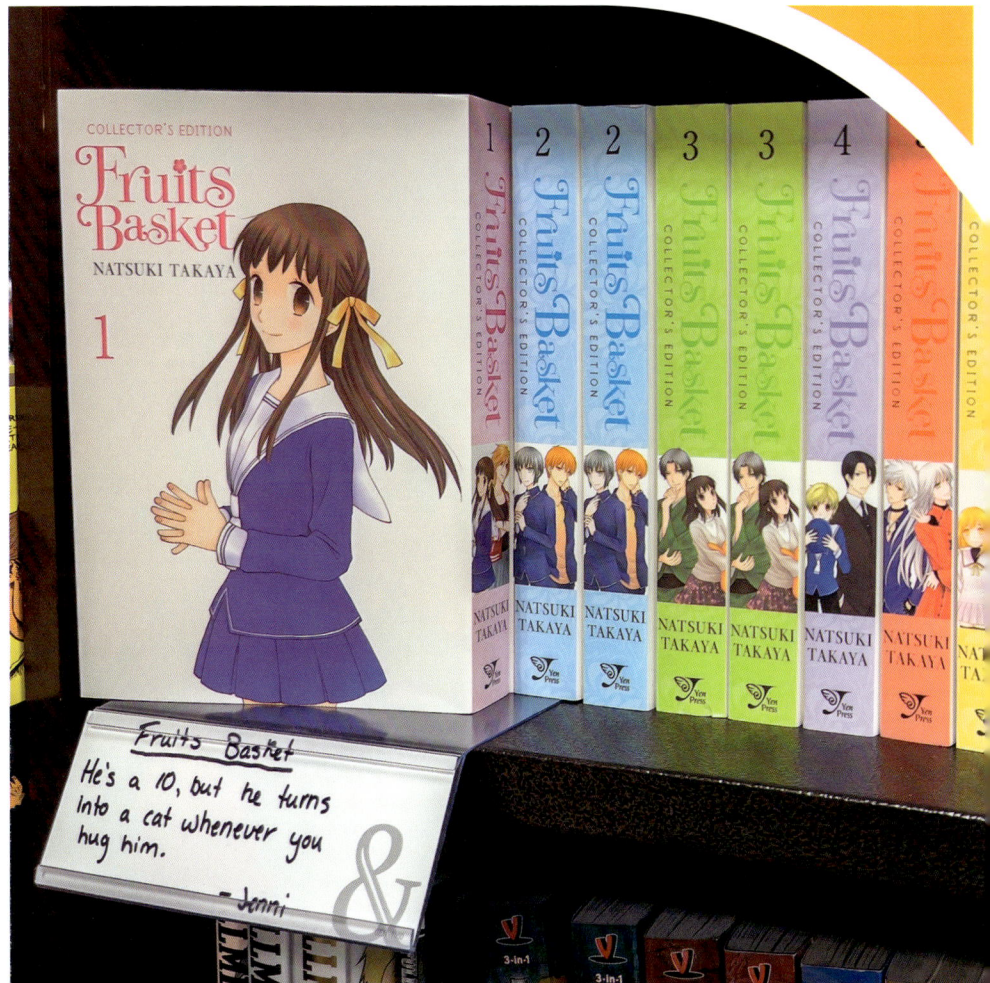

"Except," Wren interrupts, "for manga." She's the club's vice president. Wren points to the many books spread across the library's tables. She holds up *Fruits Basket*, a fantasy by Natsuki Takaya. "I'm reading this tonight," Wren says excitedly. She then grabs a sports manga called *Slam Dunk*. It was written by Takehiko Inoue. "Actually, I'm going to read a book from each genre," she decides. Into her backpack she stuffs Yukito Kishiro's *Battle Angel Alita*. This one is a sci-fi manga. "I can't wait to read all of these!"

"Don't forget to sleep," Juri says, laughing. But he knows exactly how she feels. Watching anime sparked his love for manga too. "Check out as many manga as you want. There are all kinds of genres with awesome themes." Juri fist-bumps

Part of the sports genre, Slam Dunk was created in 1990. Art from the popular series has been featured in museum exhibitions of Japanese anime and manga around the world.

all the other members as they leave. Their backpacks are filled with manga. He cannot wait to talk about more anime and manga next week.

Naruto is a manga and anime series from the shonen genre. Many fans collect action figures of the main character, who is also named Naruto.

ANIME AND MANGA GENRES

Anime is animation from Japan. Animators make anime movies and TV shows. Manga is a genre of comics. Mangakas are artists who make these comics. Anime and manga influence each other. There are many anime series based on manga. There are also manga based on existing anime.

Anime and manga are made for specific age-groups and audiences. A category of anime or manga is known as a genre. For example, shonen and shojo are genres made for teenagers. Animators and mangakas explore many themes through different genres. Each story they create may have multiple themes. The wide variety of genres and themes makes it possible for nearly everyone to find anime and manga they enjoy.

1
SHONEN AND SHOJO

Animators and mangakas create stories with their audiences in mind. For example, most kids begin by watching or reading kodomomuke. This genre is created for all genders of young children.

The characters in this genre are drawn to appeal to kids. Hello Kitty wears a big red bow. Pikachu from *Pokémon* is bright yellow with rosy cheeks. Anime and manga are also made for teenagers. Shonen and shojo are two of the most popular genres for teens.

In 2001, Pikachu from Pokémon began a long string of appearances in the Macy's Thanksgiving Day Parade.

The hero's journeys featured in My Hero Academia *and* Dragon Ball Z *inspire some fans to dress up as characters from these series at anime and manga conventions.*

THE SHONEN GENRE

Shonen is a genre based on age and gender. Boys aged 12 years or older often like this genre. Themes in shonen include action, adventure, coming of age, and friendship.

Shonen characters are heroes who work hard to learn new skills. They may gain power to win fights against villains. Anime viewers or manga readers follow the characters along a hero's journey. This theme often begins with a hero who leaves his home to go on a quest. Throughout his journey, he learns lessons as he works hard to reach his dreams. The hero defeats villains and learns lessons about growing up, such as how to be a friend or a leader. By the time he returns home, the hero has grown to become a better person.

EXAMPLES OF SHONEN

There are many popular shonen series. The anime and manga *My Hero Academia* was created by Kohei Horikoshi. He released the first manga volume in Japan in 2014. As of 2023, the manga series was still published in *Weekly Shonen Jump*.

My Hero Academia features a hero named Izuku Midoriya. Izuku and his friends want to attend superhero school. But Izuku was born without a superpower. One of the themes of this story is working together for success. The anime version of *My Hero Academia* was released in Japan in 2016.

One Piece by mangaka Eiichiro Oda first appeared in *Weekly Shonen Jump* in 1997. This manga series is about a teen named Monkey D. Luffy. Luffy wants to be the king of the pirates. But to do so, he must find the treasure known as the One Piece. Other characters help Luffy. The story's themes explore friendship. Like many manga, this one also inspired an anime.

It was released in Japan in 1999. *One Piece* won the Crunchyroll Anime Award for Best Continuing Series in 2023.

THE SHOJO GENRE

Young girls aged 12 or older often prefer the shojo genre. Themes in shojo include drama, coming of age, love, and romance.

Shojo characters explore relationships between families and friends to empower

MANGA MAGAZINES

In Japan, many manga series appear first in magazines. For example, *Weekly Shonen Jump* is a best-selling magazine made for teenage boys. *Hana to Yume* is a magazine for teenage girls. Sometimes, the manga series in magazines are published in tankoubon, which are graphic novels.

The shojo genre often explores themes of relationships. They may be between family members, friends, or romantic partners.

young girls. Shojo stories often involve characters falling in love. These romantic relationships focus on respect and trust. Characters grow as individuals. The female characters explore their identities and learn to accept themselves. Laura Neuzeth is a social media influencer. She is interested in shojo manga. Neuzeth says, "Manga in recent years has done an incredible job of celebrating and portraying different kinds of girls and women."[1]

EXAMPLES OF SHOJO

Many shojo fans enjoy reading *Orange* by Ichigo Takano. This manga was first published in Japan in 2012. The main character is eleventh grader Naho. She receives a letter from her future self. Naho assumes the letter is a joke until events mentioned in it come true. Taking the letter more seriously, she helps a new boy in school named Kakeru. Naho's future self tells her she is the only person who can save Kakeru from his sadness. This story's themes include time travel and love.

One of the most popular shojo anime is *Sailor Moon* by Naoko Takeuchi. It first appeared in manga form in Japan in 1991. The anime version followed in 1992. The main character of *Sailor Moon* is Usagi Tsukino. She is in many ways a typical 14-year-old girl. But she finds out from a cat named Luna that she is also the princess of the moon. This role means she must defend love and justice. Winning battle after battle to help her friends, Usagi gains power. She must use it to defend Earth from evil. The story explores themes of magic and identity.

Many Sailor Moon fans like the fact that its female characters rarely speak about their looks. They are much more focused on fighting evil and saving the world.

TOP 5 BEST-SELLING MANGA TITLES

Ranking	Title	Genre	Duration
1st	*One Piece* by Eiichiro Oda	Fantasy / Shonen / Action & Adventure	1997–Present
2nd	*Golgo 13* by Takao Saito	Fantasy / Shonen / Action & Adventure	1968–Present
3rd	*Case Closed / Detective Conan* by Gosho Aoyama	Fantasy / Shonen / Crime / Mystery	1994–Present
4th	*Dragon Ball* by Akira Toriyama	Fantasy / Action & Adventure	1984–Present
5th	*Doraemon* by Fujiko F. Fujio	Science Fiction / Comedy	1969–2014

Source: Suzail Ahmad. "The 14 Best-Selling Manga in History," Game Rant, April 18, 2023. https://gamerant.com.

Some of the best-selling manga titles have been in print for more than 50 years.

In both shonen and shojo, the characters grow as people. A seventh-grade student from New York noted this in an interview with a school librarian. The student said, "While manga is more . . . an animated form of reading, including more visuals than words, it demonstrates the true character development that all ages can clearly see."[2] Themes in these stories help readers and viewers understand how characters and real people change over time.

2

FANTASY AND ISEKAI

Fantasy is a popular anime and manga genre. Many fans also enjoy the subgenre isekai, which includes characters finding themselves in a new world. While there, the characters may have to complete a specific mission. Then they may return to their own world. Mangakas and animators create fantastic worlds for isekai and other fantasy stories.

THE FANTASY GENRE

The fantasy genre includes many anime and manga series. It is a category containing a huge variety of stories. Reporter Jacob H. Buchalter states, "Defining a manga as a 'fantasy' series is about the broadest descriptor one could use. It's about as bad as describing a video game as an 'action'

Many anime and manga fit into more than one genre. One Piece, for example, may be classified as both shonen and fantasy.

Spirited Away's fantastical creatures are among the reasons this anime falls within the fantasy genre.

game since almost every release out there has a lot of action in it."³

Reporter Louis Kemner explains that what unites many fantasy works is a love of the impossible. He says, "Fantasy is about what can never be, **supernatural** and fantastical things that exist only in everyone's imagination. In the best fantasy anime series, the impossible becomes very real, and that's what makes it so wonderful to watch."[4]

In fantasy anime and manga, viewers and readers follow characters on adventures. The main characters travel to magical lands. They are often normal people turned into heroes. The stories may include magical creatures and mysterious monsters. There may be future technologies, magic, and battles. The hero often saves the fantasy world.

EXAMPLES OF FANTASY

The manga *Fruits Basket* was released in Japan in 1998. The story follows 16-year-old orphan Tohru Honda. After a classmate's family invites her to live with them, she discovers the boy's family is cursed.

The family members cannot hug anyone of the opposite gender. If they do, they turn into animals. Tohru must help the family. This story's themes center on family.

Attack on Titan by Hajime Isayama is another popular fantasy series. The manga came out in 2009, and an anime adaptation followed in 2013. This story is set in an imaginary, dystopian place. In dystopian settings, characters are sad and fearful because they are mistreated. This story explores dystopian themes about war and militaries.

In *Attack on Titan*, viewers experience the fantastical world through Eren Jaeger and his friends. Titans are giant **humanoids** who eat people for no reason. To stay safe, humans stay in the city behind towering walls. One day the Titans break through

Universal Studios Japan features a 49-foot (15-m) Armored Giant from Attack on Titan.

the walls with a swift kick. A Colossal Titan murders Eren's mom. Eren seeks revenge. Tired of being attacked by the creatures, Eren and his friends fight to win their world back.

THE ISEKAI SUBGENRE

In the isekai subgenre, the main character is suddenly trapped in a new world. Characters may find themselves in magical worlds such as video games or unfamiliar places. Characters may also be trapped in different time periods. Sometimes the opposite may happen. In reverse isekai stories, a fantasy character from another world is brought to Earth.

In the new world, characters are usually more powerful. To find their way back home, they must survive adventures or quests. Important themes in isekai highlight why people make the choice to return home.

EXAMPLES OF ISEKAI

A popular isekai anime is *Spirited Away* by Hayao Miyazaki. After its 2001 release in Japan, it came to the United States in 2002.

THEMES IN STUDIO GHIBLI MOVIES

Studio Ghibli is a Japanese production company. It was founded by director Hayao Miyazaki. His films tell emotional stories about family, friendship, love, and war. Some of the stories are created first as anime. Others are manga developed into anime. No matter how they begin, the award-winning movies created by Studio Ghibli are popular with audiences worldwide.

Spirited Away *is one of the most famous isekai anime in history. It inspired many other isekai stories.*

The main character is 10-year-old Chihiro. Chihiro finds herself in a new world. She discovers a theme park where gods and spirits exist. While at the park, her parents overeat and turn into pigs. She must work hard to find her way back home and save her family. Themes in this story include family and love.

Spirited Away won an Academy Award in 2003. This award is sometimes called an Oscar. Director Hayao Miyazaki's film was the first anime to win an Oscar. It was for Best Animated Feature.

Reporter Matthew Guida wrote, "Isekai's popularity has skyrocketed, resulting in several more isekai anime adaptations."[5] For example, *Sword Art Online* is a series about a video game that traps all its players within its world. The main character, Kirito, tries to save himself and the 10,000 other players stuck in the game. Another example is *Dr. Stone*, created by Riichiro Inagaki and Boichi. Transported to a stone-age future,

In Sword Art Online, everyone is trapped in a game. Anyone who dies in the game also dies in real life.

Taiju and Senku are determined to bring technology to this stone age.

    A manga example of the isekai genre is *That Time I Got Reincarnated as a Slime*. Two mangakas, Fuse and Taiki Kawakami, tell the story about a man named Mikami. After dying, he awakes as a slime monster in a magical world filled with dragons. An unlikely hero, Mikami plans to build a new country for everyone. Mistreated by society, he especially wants to help people who feel alone. This manga was released in Japan in 2014. An anime movie adaptation arrived in 2022. The themes in this story include a focus on building community.

3

SCI-FI AND MECHA

Science fiction, or sci-fi, is a popular genre for anime and manga. Mecha is a subgenre of sci-fi. This subgenre is known for its giant robots. Technology is a common part of the sci-fi and mecha genres. Animators and mangakas imagine futuristic stories. They explore themes of good battling evil.

THE SCI-FI GENRE

Sci-fi explores stories about space travel and the future. Sci-fi stories may also include monsters, **cyborgs**, or aliens. Whatever the setting, the main character usually faces a dangerous world.

Using unique details, mangakas and animators make the sci-fi world feel real.

The popular mecha franchise Gundam includes anime, manga, video games, and more.

Characters need to navigate the mysterious worlds. The settings may be dystopian. They may also be postapocalyptic. This means the time period of the story takes place after a terrible disaster. The artists draw backgrounds of the sci-fi settings. Details often include futuristic vehicles, places, and creatures.

EXAMPLES OF SCI-FI

Battle Angel Alita is a **cyberpunk** manga. Written by Yukito Kishiro, this sci-fi manga released in Japan in 1990. Three years later, an anime adaptation aired. Themes in this manga explore identity, humanity, and war.

In the future, after The Great War, life is dangerous for humans. The people live in Scrapyard, which is the garbage dump for a

Like many other sci-fi manga, Battle Angel Alita is set in a postapocalyptic world.

rich, floating city named Zalem. Every day is a fight for survival. A scientist named Dr. Ido is devastated by the death of his daughter, Alita. He uses her body to build a cyborg. The new Alita is a cross between a human

Naoki Urasawa discusses his manga at a showing of his work in Los Angeles, California, in 2019.

and a robot. She learns that Dr. Ido is a warrior. She must save him from villains.

Pluto is a manga and an anime. It is based on Osamu Tezuka's *Astro Boy* from the 1960s. Created by Naoki Urasawa and Takashi Nagasaki, the manga came out in Japan in 2004. Directed by Toshio Kawaguchi, the sci-fi anime released internationally in 2023. Themes in this story include power, choices, and postwar **trauma**.

Pluto's main character is Gesicht. He is a humanoid detective. Gesicht is also one of the greatest giant robots. Robots and humans live in peace until a giant robot is killed. This is a huge problem. Jason Thompson stated, "In this world, robots have only recently been granted rights, and human-robot **discrimination** still exists."[6] Gesicht searches for the murderer. He discovers a giant robot named Pluto is hunting other robots. Pluto does not want robots to have equal rights. Pluto even murders humans for protecting robot rights. Gesicht must solve the case.

THE MECHA GENRE

Mecha is usually set in the future. Short for *mechanical*, the mecha genre often includes technology. It may feature computers, spaceships, or lasers. Mecha can also include space settings with **androids**, cyborgs, and giant robots.

The mecha genre is known for giant super robots or real robots. Super robots are one-of-a-kind superstars. They are usually created by scientists. They might come from ancient times. Sometimes they move on their own. Usually, humans pilot them from inside the super robot or by remote control. Real robots are also piloted by humans from inside the robot. Real robots are realistic war machines. They are built for combat.

Cell from Dragon Ball Z is one of the most popular androids in sci-fi anime. Although he is a villain, viewers can tell that Cell truly respects the story's main character, Goku.

EXAMPLES OF MECHA

Mangaka Tsutomu Nihei created *Knights of Sidonia* in 2009. Five years later, the anime aired. In this story, the audience follows a young man named Nagate. He searches for food and finds other humans who are under attack. Terrible aliens called Guana are killing humans.

To save humanity, Nagate pilots the spaceship known as Sidonia. As a knight of Sidonia, Nagate and his team search the galaxy to fight Guana. Only one weapon can stop Guana. It is a special spear called Kabizashi. Fighting for survival is an important theme in the story.

The anime *Neon Genesis Evangelion* is about human-made machines called Evangelions. The Evangelions use alien

Some of the themes found in Neon Genesis Evangelion *are freedom, choice, and responsibility.*

technology to battle giant monsters known as the Angels throughout the galaxy. The Evangelions fight the Angels to save humanity and Earth.

In this mecha anime, viewers follow 14-year-old Shinji Ikari. He has not heard from his dad in years. But one day, his dad asks him to come to Neo Tokyo-3 City. There, Shinji Ikari becomes the pilot of a robot. A member of the Evangelions, he

GENRE MIX-UP

Some mangakas and animators make old ideas seem new again. They may blend the mecha and isekai genres into one story. A robot might be sent into a new world. Directed by Yusuke Yamamoto, *Knight's & Magic* is a blended anime. Tsubasa is reborn into a medieval kingdom with robots.

fights against the Angels who are invading Earth. Themes in this story include bravery and tragedy. Directed by Hideaki Anno, it was released in Japan in 1995.

A famous mecha anime is *Mobile Suit Gundam*. It was created by director Yoshiyuki Tomino in 1979. Fans follow Amuro Ray through different battles in the One Year War. Amuro's dad is a scientist. He works for the Federation. The Earth Federation is a government that battles a group named Principality of Zeon. Amuro's dad designs mobile suits called Gundam. To protect his home colony, Amuro must fight a squad from Zeon. To win the fight, he pilots the Gundam. *Mobile Suit Gundam* contains anti-war themes.

4
SLICE OF LIFE AND SPORTS

The slice-of-life and sports genres bring real-life experiences into the world of anime and manga. This helps readers and viewers connect with the characters in these stories. Through wins and losses, characters grow as individuals. In both genres, the theme of friendship is common.

THE SLICE-OF-LIFE GENRE

The slice-of-life genre tells stories about daily experiences. Schools and homes

Shoyo Hinata is a character from the popular sports anime and manga Haikyu!! The story follows a school volleyball team.

are common settings in these stories. Characters learn as they experience the ups and downs of life. Characters make mistakes and learn to accept themselves. As they fall in love, they learn to be respectful and honest. When they fight or argue, characters learn about solving problems and being kind to others.

Within the slice-of-life genre, anime and manga stories may help audiences deal

ONE OFTEN LEADS TO THE OTHER

Audiences often move between anime and manga. Readers may miss a character after finishing a manga series. They may then watch the anime version of that series. The reverse happens too. Anime and manga keep readers connected with their favorite characters.

with issues in their own lives. Reporter Alexandra Locke says, "Slice-of-life anime are among some of the most calming and **poignant** stories. They teach valuable lessons. . . . Though they are not flashy, what they lack in action they make up for in emotional maturity and beautiful animation. There is something to be said about the way slice-of-life anime make fans feel, and that is most of their charm."[7]

EXAMPLES OF SLICE OF LIFE

A popular manga title in the slice-of-life genre is *Komi Can't Communicate*. Mangaka Tomohito Oda published this manga in Japan in 2016. The manga was adapted into an anime in 2021. Its themes include mental health and friendship.

Komi Can't Communicate details Komi's experience with anxiety. A quiet high school girl, Komi struggles with making friends. At first, she makes one friend named Tadano. He helps her meet her goal of making one hundred friends. She works hard to improve her communication skills. This effort helps her connect with people.

The manga *Satoko and Nada* was created by Yupechika. It was released in Japan in 2017. Satoko is from Japan. Nada is from Saudi Arabia. The girls meet at college as roommates. As the girls become friends, they realize how much they have in common. Themes in this story include friendship and diversity. Diversity embraces the differences between people. It shows that differences do not make one person better than another.

The First Slam Dunk *is based on* **Slam Dunk,** *one of the best-selling sports manga of all time.*

THE SPORTS GENRE

Characters also learn about life in the sports genre. Working together with teammates, players compete. They experience important lessons about winning and losing. For example, they may learn how to win without hurting others' feelings. As teammates, players develop friendships. They learn to compete while also enjoying the game they play.

EXAMPLES OF SPORTS

The First Slam Dunk is an anime by director Nobutaka Nishizawa. The movie was released in Japan in 2022. The anime is based on the manga *Slam Dunk* by Takehiko Inoue, which came out in the 1990s. The story is about a high school basketball team. Themes of hard work and competition are central to the story.

The main character is Sakuragi Hanamichi. The teenager meets a beautiful

Slam Dunk's *Kaede Rukawa* is often quiet and cold to the other players. He cares about little other than winning.

girl named Haruko Akagi. To win her heart, he joins the basketball team. Sakuragi struggles because he has never played basketball. Trying to impress Haruko as a basketball player is a challenge.

Run on Your New Legs is a manga by Wataru Midori. It was released in 2019

The slice-of-life and sports genres offer manga fans opportunities to identify with the characters and themes in the stories they read.

in Japan. The main character, Kikuzato, loses his left leg in an accident. Unable to run, he must give up soccer. Life changes when he meets an inventor who helps him use his new **prosthetic** leg. He learns to run again. Setting a new goal, he plans to win a gold medal at the 2020 Tokyo Paralympics. Determination is a key theme of the story.

Life is shown in the sports and slice-of-life genres. Readers and viewers make connections with the characters. Librarian Karina Quilanta-Garza says, "Positive representation in manga allows us to compare and contrast our stories to find commonalities and embrace differences, thus inspiring new generations of storytellers to continue to create work for future readers who want to find themselves in the literature that they read."[8]

Manga and anime stories span different genres. Mangakas and animators tell stories with important themes. Readers and viewers experience the characters' actions and motivations. They connect with the characters in different settings. Creators make anime and manga for everyone.

GLOSSARY

androids
human-like robots

cyberpunk
a subgenre of science fiction that takes place in urban societies with advanced technology

cyborgs
humans who have mechanical parts built into their bodies

discrimination
the act of treating some people well while treating others poorly because of differences between them

humanoids
creatures with human-like characteristics

poignant
emotional, deeply connected to the heart

prosthetic
a human-made device to replace a missing body part

supernatural
something that cannot be explained by natural laws or science

trauma
a terrible experience that hurts physically or emotionally

SOURCE NOTES

CHAPTER ONE: SHONEN AND SHOJO

1. Quoted in Jillian Rudes, "Representation of Girls and Women in Manga: An Interview with Laura Neuzeth," *Manga in Libraries: A Guide for Teen Librarians*," Chicago, IL: ALA Editions, 2023, p. 35.

2. Quoted in Rudes, "Representation of Girls and Women in Manga: An Interview with Laura Neuzeth," p. 58.

CHAPTER TWO: FANTASY AND ISEKAI

3. Jacob H. Buchalter, "13 Best Fantasy Manga That Do Not Have an Anime," *Game Rant*, June 14, 2023. https://gamerant.com.

4. Quoted in Wilson Cook, "Best Fantasy Manga of 2023," *Find This Best*, August 19, 2023. www.findthisbest.com.

5. Matthew Guida, "The 43 Best Isekai of All Time, Ranked," *CBR*, May 30, 2023. www.cbr.com.

CHAPTER THREE: SCI-FI AND MECHA

6. Jason Thompson, "Jason Thompson's House of 1,000 Manga—*Pluto*," *Anime News Network*, September 13, 2012. www.animenewsnetwork.com.

CHAPTER FOUR: SLICE OF LIFE AND SPORTS

7. Alexandra Locke, "The 35 Best Slice-of-Life Anime, Ranked," *CBR*, July 1, 2023. www.cbr.com.

8. Quoted in Rudes, "Representation of Girls and Women in Manga: An Interview with Laura Neuzeth," p. 43.

FOR FURTHER RESEARCH

BOOKS

Christine Ha, *Anime and Manga*. San Diego, CA: BrightPoint Press, 2021.

Patrick Macias and Samuel Sattin, *A Kid's Guide to Anime & Manga: Exploring the History of Japanese Animation and Comics*. Philadelphia, PA: Running Press Kids, 2023.

Sarah Roggio, *Anime and Manga Artists*. San Diego, CA: BrightPoint Press, 2024.

INTERNET SOURCES

"Drawn to Inspire: The Impact of Manga and Anime," *Japan House Los Angeles*, August 16, 2019. www.japanhousela.com.

"Manga Book Club Handbook," *Comic Book Legal Defense Fund*, n.d. https://cbldf.org.

Amanda Pagan, "A Beginner's Guide to Manga," *New York Public Library*, December 27, 2018. www.nypl.org.

WEBSITES

Manga in Libraries
https://mangainlibraries.com

Manga in Libraries includes lists of manga recommended by librarian Jillian Rudes.

No Flying No Tights
https://noflyingnotights.com

The No Flying No Tights website provides reviews of anime, manga, and comics.

School Library Journal Good Comics for Kids
https://goodcomicsforkids.slj.com

The *School Library Journal* Good Comics for Kids blog provides reviews, interviews, news, and previews of kids' comics for readers and fans.

INDEX

Astro Boy, 40
Attack on Titan, 28
awards, 17, 31, 33

Battle Angel Alita, 8, 38–40

Case Closed, 22
cyberpunk, 38

Detective Conan, 22
Doraemon, 22
Dr. Stone, 33–35
Dragon Ball, 22

fantasy, 8, 22, 24–35
Fruits Basket, 8, 27–28

Golgo 13, 22

Hana to Yume, 17
Hello Kitty, 12

isekai, 30–35, 46

Knight's & Magic, 46
Knights of Sidonia, 44
kodomomuke, 12
Komi Can't Communicate, 51–52

mangakas, 10–11, 12, 16, 24, 35, 36, 37, 44, 46, 51, 57
mecha, 42, 44–47
Mobile Suit Gundam, 47
My Hero Academia, 15–16

Neon Genesis Evangelion, 44–46

One Piece, 16–17, 22
Orange, 19–20

Pluto, 40–41
Pokémon, 12

Run on Your New Legs, 55–56

Sailor Moon, 20
Satoko and Nada, 52
science fiction, 8, 22, 36–41
shojo, 11, 13, 17–22
shonen, 11, 13–17
Slam Dunk, 8, 54–55
slice of life, 48–52, 57
Spirited Away, 6, 31–33
sports, 48, 53–57
Studio Ghibli, 31
Sword Art Online, 33–35

That Time I Got Reincarnated as a Slime, 35

Weekly Shonen Jump, 16, 17

IMAGE CREDITS

Cover: © Timur1985/Shutterstock Images
5: © Colleen Michaels/Shutterstock Images
7: © Colleen Michaels/Shutterstock Images
9: © Imaginechina Limited/Alamy
10: © Aisyaqilumaranas/Shutterstock Images
13: © gary718/Shutterstock Images
14: © Stephen Chung/Alamy Live News/Alamy
18: © djvstock/iStockphoto
21: © BrendanHunter/iStockphoto
22: © Red Line Editorial
25: © Tuchong/Imaginechina Limited/Alamy
26: © Studio Ghibli/AJ Pics/Alamy
29: © Usa-Pyon/Shutterstock Images
32: © Studio Ghibli/Maximum Film/Alamy
34: © Arturo Vazquez/Alamy
37: © Black Wang/Alamy
39: © Moviestore Collection Ltd/Alamy
40: © Cronos/Hollywood News/Alamy
43: © Christian Lademann/LademannMedia/Alamy
45: © TV Tokyo/AJ Pics/Alamy
49: © kuremo/Panther Media GmbH/Alamy
53: © Dandelion Animation Studios/Toei Animation/Album/Alamy
55: © cfg1978/Shutterstock Images
56: © Diganime/Shutterstock Images

ABOUT THE AUTHOR

Danielle L. DeFauw, PhD, is a professor of reading and language arts at the University of Michigan–Dearborn. She dreams of publishing middle grade and young adult novels about healing, hope, and heart. She loves to empower readers to live through characters' experiences. DeFauw loves the power of story in all forms.